BY VALERIE BODDEN

This edition copyright © Franklin Watts 2014
338 Euston Road
London NW1 3BH

Franklin Watts Australia
Level 17/207 Kent Street
Sydney NSW 2000

First published by Creative Education
P.O. Box 227, Mankato, Minnesota 56002
Creative Education is an imprint of The Creative Company
www.thecreativecompany.us
Copyright © 2010 Creative Education

ISBN 978 1 4451 3037 8
Dewey number: 919.4'3
A CIP catalogue record for this book
is available from the British Library.

Printed in China

Franklin Watts is a division of
Hachette Children's Books,
an Hachette UK company.
www.hachette.co.uk

Design and production by The Design Lab
Art direction by Rita Marshall

Photographs by Alamy (NASA), Jay Ireland and Georgienne
Bradley/Bradley Ireland Productions, Corbis (David
Ball, Robert Garvey, Paul A. Souders, Penny Tweedie,
Bill Varie, Lawson Wood), Dreamstime (Banol2007,
Goodolga, Ingvars, Mwookie, Sjm1123, Thomasgulla)

Every attempt has been made to clear copyright.
Should there be any inadvertent omission, please
contact the publisher for rectification.

GREAT PLANET EARTH
GREAT BARRIER REEF

W
FRANKLIN WATTS
LONDON • SYDNEY

Great Barrier Reef

AUSTRALIA

The Great Barrier Reef is the biggest **coral** reef system in the world. A coral reef is an underwater ridge made up of coral. The Great Barrier Reef is found in the sea surrounding the **continent** of Australia.

An island on the Great Barrier Reef. Coral reefs are usually found in warm, shallow seas.

GREAT PLANET EARTH 6 GREAT BARRIER REEF

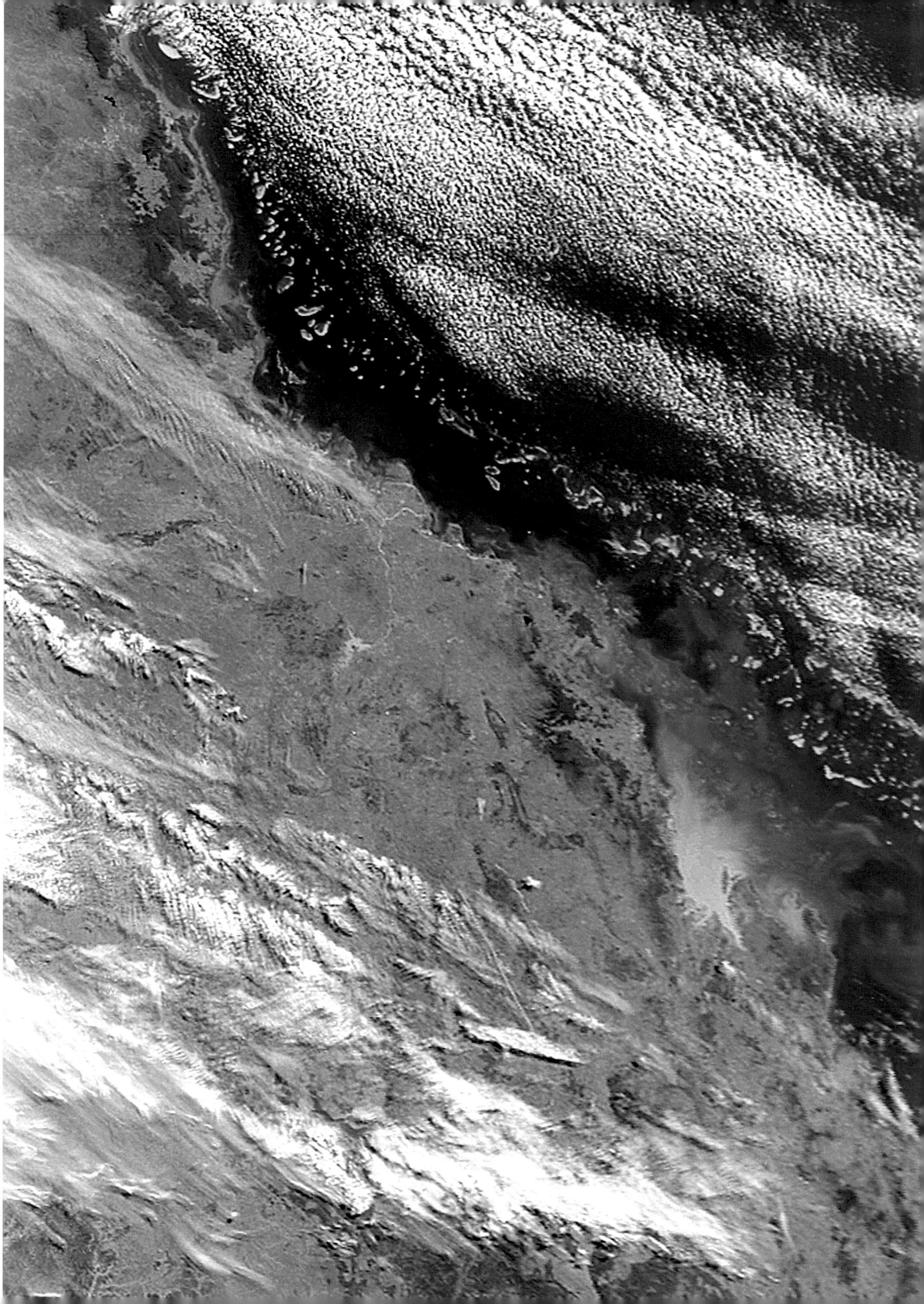

Almost 3,000 different coral reefs make up the Great Barrier Reef system. It stretches along the Australian coastline for more than 2,300 kilometres.

The Great Barrier Reef is so big that it can be seen from space. Here it can be seen as the blue/green shading around the **coast** of Australia.

The Great Barrier Reef was formed by tiny animals called coral polyps (*POH-lips*). Coral polyps attach themselves to the **skeletons** of hard coral. Then they make a skeleton around themselves. When the polyps die, their skeletons become another layer of the coral reef.

Some types of coral polyp are hard (above), but other kinds are soft (right). Only hard coral polyps build stony skeletons.

More than 400
different kinds of
coral make up the
Great Barrier Reef.

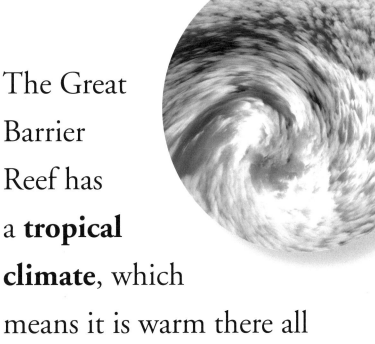

The Great Barrier Reef has a **tropical climate**, which means it is warm there all year round. Sometimes there are big storms called cyclones (above). There are many small towns on the coast near the reef.

Visitors to the Great Barrier Reef often stay at resorts on the shore in towns like Port Douglas (left).

Colourful fish swim around the Great Barrier Reef. Starfish, eels and jellyfish live near the reef, too. So do sharks and sea turtles.

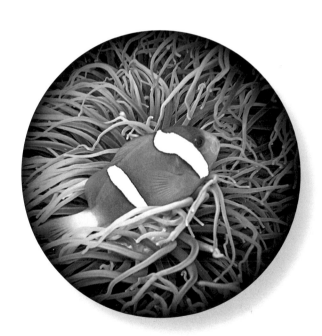

Clownfish (above) and sea turtles (right) share the reef's waters. The rich **ecosystem** of the reef provides them with food to eat.

Over 1,500 different kinds of fish swim around the Great Barrier Reef.

Mangrove swamps are found near the Great Barrier Reef. They are important ecosystems for many different types of animal. Large birds such as herons and egrets find food in the swamps. Outside the reef, whales and dolphins swim in the deep water.

Humpback whales (left) and egrets (above) live close to the Great Barrier Reef.

Australian **Aborigines** (*ab-uh-RIJ-uh-neez*) have lived near the Great Barrier Reef for thousands of years. They first explored the reef in canoes and used its rich waters for fishing and hunting. The first Europeans found the Great Barrier Reef around 250 years ago.

Australian Aborigines (right) have a special bond with the Great Barrier Reef.

The crown-of-thorns starfish hurts coral reefs by eating coral polyps.

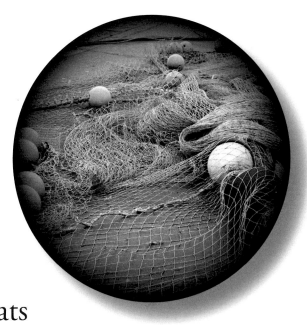

Today, there are many threats to the Great Barrier Reef, both natural and man-made. Fishing nets (above) damage coral, while shipwrecks **pollute** the water and **poison** fish. But the biggest threat is **global warming**, as rising sea temperatures damage the fragile reef ecosystem.

Crown-of-thorns starfish (left) are blamed for damaging many parts of the Great Barrier Reef.

Every year, millions of people visit the Great Barrier Reef. Some dive in the reef's waters. Others take boat trips to the reef's remote islands. Visitors are always amazed by this wonderful underwater world!

Scuba diving is a great way to see the colourful coral of the Great Barrier Reef up close.

If the water they live in gets too hot, coral can lose their bright colours.

There are lots of types of coral. They can look like branches, tentacles or even giant brains!

Aborigines the people who have lived in a place for the longest time

climate the usual weather in a place

coast the edge of the land closest to the water

continent one of Earth's seven big pieces of land

coral a hard, stony material made from the skeletons of groups of living animals called coral polyps

ecosystem all the living things in a place, such as a coral reef

global warming a gradual rise in the Earth's temperature

mangrove a tropical tree, found near water

poison to make a living thing sick

pollute to make the air, water or earth dirty

skeletons animals' hard outer coverings or the bones inside their bodies

tropical hot and humid

Read More about It

Inside a Coral Reef by Carole Telford (Heinemann, 2007)

What Can I See? Coral Reef (TickTock Books, 2006)

Index